READING THE REVIEWS

I sit at my computer reading camera reviews. When I type in "digital cameras" at www.cnet.com, I pull up over 500 search results. Yikes! I decide to search for 3MP cameras with 3X Optical Zoom and priced at less than $300.

My list of results is still fairly long, so I decide to sort my results by reviews. I want to know which cameras got top-notch marks for image quality and ease of use. I read the reviews on www.cnet.com, then decide I should look at other sites as well. I read camera reviews on www.dpreview.com, www.pcphoto.com, and www.epinions.com. I make a list of cameras with good to excellent ratings for image quality and ease of use.

VISITING A LOCAL STORE

I decide to take a field trip to a local store that sells electronics. (Yes, I'm the blonde wearing red shoes that you spotted at the digital camera counter.) Now that I've read the reviews, I want to go and touch the digital cameras so I can see how they feel in my hands.

Are they bulky or light? How big are they REALLY? Will I feel comfortable holding a camera the size of a credit card? Are the switches easy to use? How quickly does a certain camera power up?

Believe me, I'm happy I've done my research before walking into the store. The product information cards on each camera don't tell me much. And the store clerk who walks over to "help" me seems intent on selling me the most expensive camera on display.

As I'm playing with one of the cameras, a man approaches and tells me he just got a Minolta Dimage XT for Christmas and it takes great photographs. I make a mental note to ask my friends and family members which digital cameras they currently use and what they like and dislike about them.

When I ask around the office, managing editor Marianne Madsen gives the thumbs up to her Pentax Optio S, while assistant editor Lori Fairbanks mentions that she loves her new Sony Cyber-shot DSC-10.

ATTENDING A CONSUMER SHOW

My search for the "perfect" digital camera for scrapbooking leads me to the Consumer Electronics Show in Las Vegas. I chat with several companies and am pleased to discover that Kodak, Epson, Hewlett-Packard, Canon, Casio, Sony, Olympus and others are committed to making "lifestyle" digital cameras so that memories are easy to capture and share.

Supplies used in article design. *Patterned papers:* K-I Memories (green) and Lasting Impressions for Paper (yellow); *Letter stickers:* SEI; *Bookplates:* Making Memories; *Black brads:* Boxer Scrapbook Productions; *Metal frame:* Scrapworks; *Clear circle snap:* Halo; *Green tacks:* Chatterbox; *Photo corners:* Canson; *Fonts:* Century Gothic, Microsoft and Hootie!, downloaded from www.free-typewriter-fonts.com; *Other:* String and machine stitching.

SHOPPING FOR BARGAINS

After I've narrowed my list, I check out sites like www.*pricegrabber.com* to find the best prices on digital cameras. (Be sure to include shipping costs when you do this.) I also flip through the Sunday newspaper ads to look for prices at my local stores. I'm surprised to find that many advertisements don't list specific model numbers!

SHARING MY FINDINGS

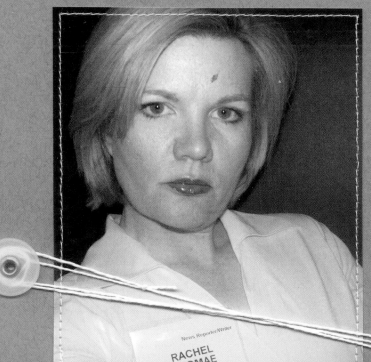

After doing my research, I call my friend Angela and start telling her about megapixels and optical zoom. She stops me mid-sentence and says, "Rachel, just tell me what digital camera to buy!" Turn the page to read about my top four picks.

Pentax Optio S

Fits in an Altoids tin, good image quality, excellent feature set. Includes several shooting modes to enhance your photographs.

The stylish 3.2 megapixel OptioS is so small it can actually fit into an empty Altoids tin! The camera's powerful 3X optical zoom lens offers high resolution and a low level of distortion. But don't let the size fool you—this small camera delivers a big punch with its shooting modes (standard, picture, night scene, movie, 3-D, panorama assist, digital filters, and user) and picture modes (landscape, flower, portrait, self-portrait, surf & snow, autumn color, and sunset). The OptioS can also record movie clips with sound up to 30 seconds in length at 12 frames per second.

Suggested retail price: $299
For more details, visit *www.pentax.com* or see your local dealer.

Sony Cyber-shot DSC-P8

Compact, fast shooting, easy to use. You might also like the Sony Cyber-shot PSC-72.

The Sony Cyber-shot DSC-P8 combines exceptional image quality with compact design, delivering 3.2 megapixel resolution with a 3X optical lens and intelligent features. The camera includes special auto-focus technology for sharply focused shots (in low-light conditions as well). Capture up to 16 frames in a row—terrific for getting that shot of your toddler on the go or your teen on the soccer field. You can also capture audio/video MPEG clips, plus enjoy a lightning-fast USB 2.0 interface.

Suggested retail price: $299
For more details, visit *www.sony.com* or see your local dealer.

Canon PowerShot A70

Ultracompact, solid image quality, speedy performance. Includes enhanced Movie Mode for clips up to three minutes.

The Canon PowerShot A70 (3.2 megapixel) is an ultra-compact, AA-battery powered model with high-end features: aluminum alloy exterior, 3X optical zoom lens, five-point autofocus system, enhanced Movie Mode with sound for clips up to three minutes, close focus to two inches, and a full range of exposure modes. It's compatible with an optional waterproof housing unit as well as supplementary wide-angle, telephoto, and macro converters for added flexibility.

Suggested retail price: $299
For more details, visit *www.canon.com* or see your local dealer.

Minolta Dimage XT

Extremely compact, good image quality, quick shutter. You might also like the Minolta Dimage Xi.

The Minolta Dimage XT accurately captures fine lines and intricate details with its 3.2 megapixel lens. Get photo-quality printouts as large as 8" x 10" at 300 dpi. Minolta's sophisticated folded optics keep the camera's design ultra-slim since they eliminate the standard protruding zoom lens. The 3X optical zoom adjusts internally—you can get within six inches of your subject. With the XT's built-in flash system, choose from a host of selectable modes like Night Portrait, Autoflash, Autoflash with red-eye reduction, Fill Flash and Flash Cancel to ensure that flash photos come out looking more natural.

Suggested retail price: $299
For more details, visit *www.minolta.com* or see your local dealer.

the scoop on

Printers

Here's what my investigation uncovered

*A*s a child, my heroine was Nancy Drew.

I always wanted to be the girl who solved the mystery, cracked the case and deciphered the secret code. After college, I actually interviewed for a job with a top-secret government agency.

My aspirations to work undercover were dashed when I didn't get the job. To console myself, I penned a '40s-inspired mystery/romance that became my first published story.

Although I haven't dabbled in mystery fiction for several years, I still dream at times about being an undercover agent. When editor-in-chief Tracy White asked me to find which photo printers were truly best for scrapbookers, I accepted quicker than you could say "Bond, James Bond."

Pages by **Becky Higgins**

Article by **Rachel Thomae**

To conduct my investigation, I spent hours wandering the aisles of electronics stores. I talked with dozens of salespeople and read numerous printer reviews online. I even traveled to the Consumer Electronics Show in Las Vegas to talk with manufacturers about printer technology.

Mission: Printer Confidential

My mission? Should I choose to accept it, Tracy said I would need to:

- Learn about photo printers for scrapbookers.
- Track down the longest-lasting inks available.
- Find printers that can print 12" x 12" scrapbook pages.
- Investigate the secrets to buying a quality photo printer.

Never one to pass up a worthy challenge, I accepted the assignment. My findings follow.

Ink Intelligence

Psst, come over here for a second. See these "third-party" inks? You know, the generic cartridges that fit your printer? I'm excited about the price but have always wondered if they're really a bargain.

Here are my findings: I requested reports from Wilhelm Imaging Research, an independent laboratory that tests inks for image permanence and fade resistance. The lab data concludes that some third-party inks will cause my photographs to start fading in as little as *six months*! Is the cost of saving money on ink worth it? Not to me!

The Facts on Fade Resistance

Want to know how long your photographs will last before fading occurs? The following results are for photographs under glass in lighted conditions (for example, a photograph that you frame and hang on your living-room wall). Fade resistance increases for photographs stored properly in closed scrapbook albums.

Pages by Becky Higgins. **Supplies** *Patterned papers:* Doodlebug Design (dots) and ScripScraps (blue woven); *Letter stickers:* SEI; *Brads:* Karen Foster Design; *Snaps:* Chatterbox; *Circle punches:* Emagination Crafts (large) and McGill (medium); *Photo corners:* Canson (paper) and Making Memories (woven); *Computer fonts:* CK Typewriter (headings), "Fresh Fonts" CD, *Creating Keepsakes;* Garamond (body text), Microsoft Word; *Pop dots:* All Night Media; *Other:* Thread and staples. *Ideas to note:* Becky used Accu-Cut Systems' paper file to add an aged look to the patterned papers. All photos were printed on the HP Photosmart 245.

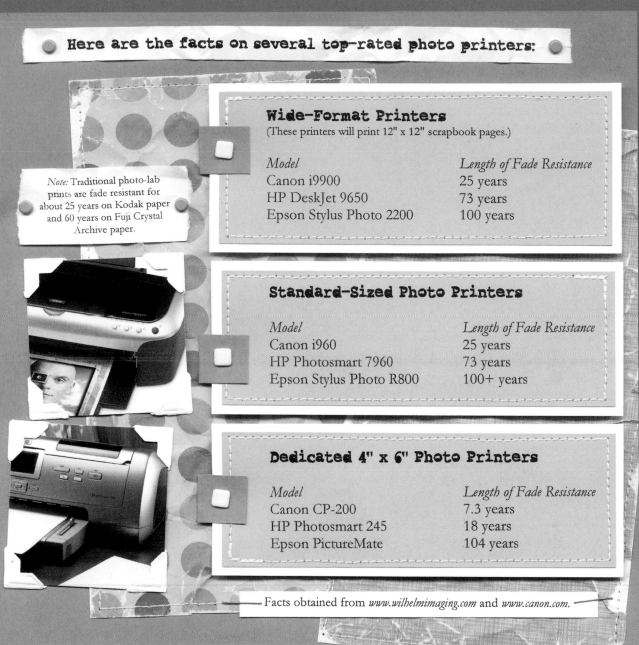

Here are the facts on several top-rated photo printers:

Wide-Format Printers
(These printers will print 12" x 12" scrapbook pages.)

Model	Length of Fade Resistance
Canon i9900	25 years
HP DeskJet 9650	73 years
Epson Stylus Photo 2200	100 years

Note: Traditional photo-lab prints are fade resistant for about 25 years on Kodak paper and 60 years on Fuji Crystal Archive paper.

Standard-Sized Photo Printers

Model	Length of Fade Resistance
Canon i960	25 years
HP Photosmart 7960	73 years
Epson Stylus Photo R800	100+ years

Dedicated 4" x 6" Photo Printers

Model	Length of Fade Resistance
Canon CP-200	7.3 years
HP Photosmart 245	18 years
Epson PictureMate	104 years

Facts obtained from *www.wilhelmimaging.com* and *www.canon.com*.

The Paper Trail

Are you ever tempted to pick up a generic brand of photo paper for your printer? I'll confess—I've done it before. But I won't make that mistake again, and here's why.

Tests show that photographs printed with Hewlett-Packard inks on the company's Premium Photo paper will resist fading for 73 years. Take those same inks, use a generic photo paper, and the results change *dramatically*, from 73 years to 2 years. Yikes! As a scrapbooker, my memories (and my photographs) are priceless, and I want them to last as long as possible.

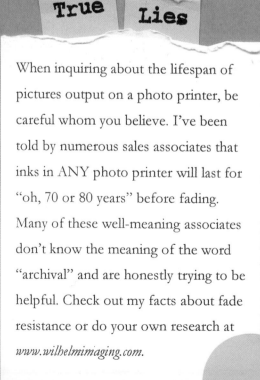

Price check! When you budget for your new printer, don't forget that you'll be paying for more than just the printer. Factor in the costs of ink, photo paper and maybe even a USB cable. Some manufacturers only partially fill the ink cartridges that come installed in your new printer. If you plan to print a lot of photographs, you may need to stock up on ink.

Don't forget to comparison shop online for the best prices on printers (check out sites like *www.pricegrabber.com* for quick and easy price comparisons). If you buy a printer with a rebate, be sure you get the proper receipts from the store clerk, and don't forget to submit your rebate forms!

True Lies

When inquiring about the lifespan of pictures output on a photo printer, be careful whom you believe. I've been told by numerous sales associates that inks in ANY photo printer will last for "oh, 70 or 80 years" before fading. Many of these well-meaning associates don't know the meaning of the word "archival" and are honestly trying to be helpful. Check out my facts about fade resistance or do your own research at *www.wilhelmimaging.com.*

Cracking the Code

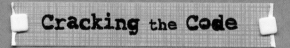

Let me fill you in on a little secret about HP printers. If you want color prints that last 73+ years without noticeable fading, buy a printer that uses the HP 58 photo cartridge. If you use the HP 57 tri-color cartridge, your prints will start to fade in about 18 years.

If you buy an HP printer, read the specs carefully. If you're looking for an all-in-one or multifunction printer (print, fax, scan and copy), you'll be happy to know that Hewlett-Packard's PSC 2410 Photosmart printer (retail price: $299) uses the HP 58 ink cartridge.

Shades of Gray

Photos by Becky Higgins

HP has a special gray photo cartridge (HP 59) that you can use in any HP Photosmart printer. This proprietary ink from HP produces better quality black-and-white photographs with true shades of gray, vivid whites and deep, rich blacks. Prints from this cartridge resist fading for 115 years.

Hostage Situation

I recently visited a local electronics store to check out a new printer. It wasn't on the shelf. I asked a sales associate if her store planned to carry this particular model. She revealed that the printer was in stock—in the store's back room.

Her store's policy? Don't display the new printers until the older models are sold out. Lesson learned: If the printer you want to buy isn't on the shelf, ask a sales associate to check the entire store inventory for you.

Rachel Confesses

I bought a photo printer last Christmas. I needed something inexpensive that would produce good quality prints for three mini-albums I'd decided to make as last-minute gifts.

I bought the Canon i560 for about $100. The fade resistance on this printer is rated at about 25 years, comparable to the longevity of traditional lab prints on Kodak paper. I'm pleased with the quality of the prints from this printer, but my next photo printer will have archival ink that lasts much longer.

Super Secrets
under
Lock and Key

At the Consumer Electronics Show, I was one of the first writers to preview the new PictureMate printer by Epson. This is a great printer for scrapbookers! First, the photographs have been tested at over 100 years for fade resistance. Second, the cost per print is about $0.29 (including photo paper and ink). Last, the printer only costs $199. The standalone printer (it doesn't need to be hooked up to your computer) is portable, easy to use and compatible with a variety of different memory cards.

Want more information or have a question about a printer I haven't covered here? The following links will help you conduct your own investigation.

Cyber-Detective Checklist

Printer Companies
Canon • www.canonusa.com
Epson • www.epson.com
Hewlett-Packard • www.hp.com

Fade Resistance Data
www.wilhelmimaging.com

Printer Reviews
www.cnet.com
www.epinions.com

Photo Printer Buying Guides
www.pcworld.com
www.pcmag.com

Mystery Solved

Wondering which printers I'd recommend to my frie nds who scrapbook? The Following are my choices.

*Wide-Format Printers

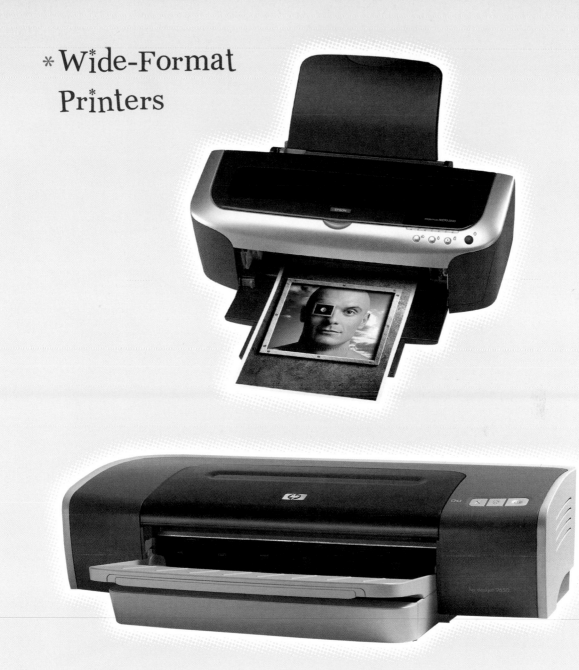

Epson Stylus Photo 2200

Perfect for scrapbookers who need archival images that will resist fading for up to 90 years, this high-speed, ink-jet printer makes it easy to create long-lasting photos and artwork on a variety of media up to 13" x 44". The Epson Stylus Photo 2200 comes with an easy-to-use roll paper holder and automatic cutter for a quick, simple way to create borderless 4" x 6" photos.

Retail price: $699
Fade resistance: 90 years
Web site: *www.epson.com*

HP DeskJet 9650

This affordable wide-format printer offers both text and photo-quality printing up to 13" x 19". Create borderless prints on media up to 11" x 17". With up to 4800 x 1200 optimized color print dpi, you'll get quality long-lasting prints. This printer includes both USB and parallel port connectivity.

Retail price: $399
Fade resistance: 73+ years
Web site: *www.hp.com*

* Photo Printers

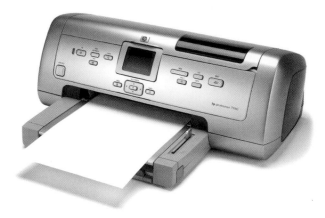

HP Photosmart 7960

The HP Photosmart 7960 includes a built-in LCD screen that lets you preview and edit images before printing. You can also print directly from digital media or an HP Direct Print digital camera. This fast photo printer utilizes HP's eight-ink technology to produce high-quality prints in both color and black and white.

Retail price: $299
Fade resistance: 73 years
Web site: *www.hp.com*

Epson Stylus Photo R800

The Epson Stylus Photo R800 is the world's first printer with 1.5-picoliter ink droplets and up to 5760 x 1440 optimized dots per inch. It provides eight individual cartridges, including matte black ink and a unique gloss optimizer. The Epson UltraChrome Hi-Gloss pigment inks deliver long-lasting portraits, landscapes and more on a variety of media, including inkjet-printable CDs, DVDs and 4" and 8.3" roll paper.

Retail price: $399
Fade resistance: 100+ years
Web site: *www.epson.com*

* Dedicated 4" x 6" Printer

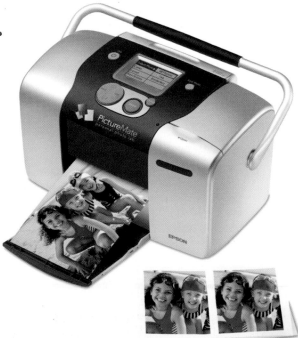

Epson PictureMate

With quick, one-touch printing, the PictureMate is like having a personal photo lab in the comfort of your own home. At about 29 cents per print, costs are comparable to having your pictures printed at a traditional lab. PictureMate photos will last longer than all the alternatives available today (even traditional lab prints).

Retail price: $199
Fade resistance: 100+ years
Web site: *www.epson.com*

SCANTASTIC!

Scanning Solutions for Scrapbookers

Have you ever seen the movie *Multiplicity*, in which actor Michael Keaton is given the opportunity to create duplicate copies of himself? I've got to admit that I'd love to have duplicates of myself to clean house, do laundry and cook dinner! And how about another Rachel who could spend all of her time creating stunning scrapbook pages?

Oh well—a girl can dream! Although I can't duplicate myself, I'm pleased that I can use my scanner to create duplicate copies of my favorite photographs. My scanner appeals to different parts of my scrapbooking personality: the Scrapbooking Mom, who likes to stitch and share pages; the Family Photographer, who likes to color correct and restore heritage photographs; and the Scrapbook Artist, who likes to be creative on her layouts. In this article, I don my "Ms. Techno Savvy" hat once again as I share my favorite scrapbook scanning solutions with you.

Pages by
Becky Higgins

Article by
Rachel Thomae

[Rachel #1]
Ms. Scrapbooking Mom

As a scrapbooking mom, one of my favorite things to do is share my completed pages with my friends and family members. In the past, I've "stitched" my 12"x12" pages together with Adobe Photoshop, then e-mailed my pages to family members. Here are a couple of new options for scanning and sharing your layouts.

12"x12" Scanners

The bad news? There isn't a 12"x12" scanner on the market today. The good news? You can buy a size A3 scanner, which has a scanning area of 11.7" x 17" (translation: it will scan almost all of your 12"x12" page). However, most large-format scanners cost several thousand dollars. I discovered the Mustek A3 scanner at *www.provantage.com* for $149.

● An Easy Stitching Solution

Scanning and stitching layouts can be time-consuming and frustrating. If you're looking for a simple stitching program, I suggest ArcSoft Panorama Maker, which makes scanning and stitching as easy as scanning both sides of your layout and then choosing the "stitch" command (no complicated merging and flattening required!). You can even download a free trial version of this program at *www.arcsoft.com*.

[Rachel #2]
Ms. Techno Savvy

To keep my title of "Ms. Techno Savvy," I read dozens of scanner reviews and sorted through scanner terminology for you. Here's the information you'll find helpful when choosing a new scanner.

Two Things to Know About Scanners

When purchasing a scanner to duplicate, restore and print photographs, you'll need to remember two terms: bit depth and optical resolution. Here's what each term means:

Optical Resolution

Look for at least 4800x1200 dpi color resolution. This will allow you to create poster-size prints of your favorite photos and will improve color reproduction in your photographs.

Bit Depth

Look for at least 48-bit color. This will allow you to capture trillions of colors for true-to-life color and accurate highlights and shadows.

Want More Detailed Info?

Looking for detailed scanner reviews? Check out these sites!

Tip: Before reading a review, check the date that the review first appeared in print. Scanner technology is changing rapidly, and products reviewed in past years may no longer be the most up-to-date technology available.

www.cnet.com

www.zdnet.com

www.pcmag.com

www.pcworld.com

[Rachel #3]
Ms. Family Photographer

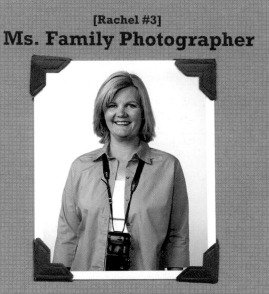

My photographs are important to me, and I want my future generations to enjoy them as much as I do! The "photo preservationist" in me is dedicated to saving and restoring my photographs. Here's how today's scanners can help you preserve your precious photographs.

Photo Magic

Today's photo scanners include technology to help you not only copy old photographs but improve them. How exciting is that? Imagine a scanner that can remove scratches and cracks from damaged photographs and negatives (no extra photo editing required) and restore faded colors in old photographs. Look for Digital Ice technology featured on scanners from Microtek and Epson and for FARE technology featured in Canon scanners.

Rescue Those Slides

So, you've inherited an old box of slides from your parents, and you want to turn the slides into prints. How do you do it without a negative? Scanners such as the Canon i9100 include "batch scan" technology. All you have to do is place your slides on the scanner bed and hit the scan button. The scanning software recognizes and saves each slide scan as an individual image. You can then create prints from your scans. Amazing!

The Little Black Slip

When scanning bulky items, it's almost impossible to get your scanner lid to close completely. Instead of trying to force the lid closed, go to a discount store and buy a short black slip (yes, from the lingerie department!). Place the slip over your scanner lid to keep light from creeping in during your scanning process.

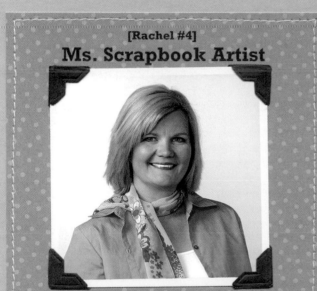

[Rachel #4]
Ms. Scrapbook Artist

I love being creative and trying new things. My scanner is a great way to scan all kinds of objects (fabric swatches, colorful crayons, clothing tags and more) into my computer! After you scan, remember that you can change the color of the item you've scanned with your photo-editing software. Here are a couple of tips to enhance your scanning creativity.

Scan a Fish?

Remember that you can scan almost anything. (I had a friend who once scanned a fish her husband caught at the lake—really! Yes, the fish was dead.) Just be careful to keep your scanner bed clean and don't let it get scratched. Consider putting items such as glass marbles in a clear photo frame or putting a piece of plastic wrap on the scanner bed before scanning in sharp objects.

Want seamless, stress-free scanning?

Try one of the following scanners, hand-picked by Rachel.

Mustek ScanExpress A3 USB
- 300 x 600 dpi resolution
- 48-bit color depth
- A3-sized scanning (11.7" x 17")
- Affordable large-format scanner

Retail price: **$149**
www.mustek.com

* Priced Under $150

MicroTek ScanMaker i320
- 4800 x 2400 dpi
- 48-bit color depth
- Digital Ice technology
- Automatic color restoration

Retail price: **$149**
www.microtek.com

*Speedy Auto-feed

HP Scanjet 5530 Photosmart
- 2400 x 4800 dpi resolution
- 48-bit color depth
- Automatic photo feeder
- Scan 24 photos in five minutes

Retail price: **$229**
Web site: *www.hp.com*

*Photo Fix Technology

Epson Perfection 4870 Photo
- 4800 x 9600 dpi resolution
- 48-bit color depth
- Digital Ice technology for film and photo prints
- Epson Photo Easy Photo Fix technology

Retail price: **$449**
www.epson.com

CanonScan 9900F Color Image Scanner
- 3200 x 6400 dpi resolution
- 48-bit color depth
- Batch scan 24 negative frames
- FARE technology (film automatic retouching and enhancement)

Retail price: **$399.99**
www.canon.com

Computer Scrapbookers

I was excited to see the names of at least three computer scrapbookers on the list of recent CK Hall of Fame winners and honorable mentions. Here, three scrapbookers share their favorite ways to get the most from their scanners.

Glenda Van Engelen

2004 Hall of Fame
Honorable Mention

"I use my scanner all the time to enlarge photographs. When I couldn't find the negative to make a copy of one of my favorite pictures of my daughter, I scanned my original print at a high resolution and printed a copy to scrapbook."

Rhonna Farrer

2004 CK Hall of
Fame Winner

"I like to use my scanner to scan in interesting things, such as intricate old keys. I scan them in, manipulate them in Photoshop 7.0 and use them as page accents on my computer-generated layouts."

Rhonda Stark

2004 CK Hall of
Fame Winner

"I use my scanner to scan photographs and archive them on CD. I also like to scan photographs where I have no negatives. In addition, by scanning my photographs, I can modify them: change them to black and white or sepia and/or enlarge them."

scanner stitching made easy

Try our handy steps and tips

Just the other day, my friend Monica turned to me and said, "I want to share my layout with someone electronically, but I'm going crazy! My 12" x 12" pages don't fit on my scanner, so I'm trying to computer stitch them together. Now my layout looks crooked, the colors don't match, and the images are all blurry. Help!"

If you've experienced frustration while scanning and stitching your 12" x 12" layouts, don't worry. You're not alone. In a few simple steps, I was able to teach Monica how to easily stitch her layouts together—and I'll teach you the same process. Ready to get started? Here's how.

The Value of Stitching

Let's say you've created a beautiful 12" x 12" scrapbook page. You'd like to send it to *Creating Keepsakes* (see top of page 261), enter it in an online contest, or e-mail it to your family members. You've been asked to scan the page and submit it electronically, but you don't have a 12" x 12" scanner.

That's where stitching software comes in handy. How does it work? You scan the right-hand and left-hand sides of your layout separately. You then use the software to "stitch" both sides of your layout into one image. Done properly, your final image will look almost as if

BY RACHEL THOMAE

NEED MORE HELP?
If you own an Epson scanner, you'll find a tutorial just for scrapbookers at *www.printlabseries.com*

you've scanned your original 12" x 12" page.

Stitching is also helpful when you want to share your two-page layouts (8½" x 11" or 12" x 12") with friends. Scan each page, stitch them together, and e-mail the two-page layout. You can also use stitching software to create your own panoramic pictures by stitching several photographs together.

Stitching, Step by Step

You can easily find many brands of scanners and types of stitching programs. I use Adobe Photoshop to scan and stitch my pages. The stitching process will vary slightly depending on your scanner and your software. Be sure to check your software manual for hints.

When you scan an image for e-mailing or to place it on a web site, scan it at a low resolution, such as 72 dpi (dots per inch). If you want to print your scrapbook pages, scan at a higher resolution, such as 300 dpi.

Here's how to scan, then stitch, a layout:

❶ Place your layout on the scanner. *Tip:* Make sure your layout is lined up against either the right- or left-hand scanning area. Use the ruler guides on your scanner to make sure the layout is positioned straight.

❷ Scan the left-hand side of your layout. Save it as a .jpg file, such as *Spring1.jpg.*

❸ Scan the right-hand side of your layout. (Make sure you scan a portion of the left-hand side as well. This is where you'll stitch the two halves of your layout together.) Save it as a .jpg file, such as *Spring2.jpg.*

❹ Go to File>New to open up a blank workspace. Fill in the width, height and resolution on the new file screen. (I use width=14", height=14" and resolution=72 dpi). Name your new image, such as *SpringFinal.jpg.*

❺ Select and copy your left-hand

image. Paste it into your new canvas.

❻ Select and copy your right-hand image. Paste it into your new canvas.

❼ Select the move tool. Drag and drop your scanned images so they overlap along a shared area.

❽ Merge the images together. (I use Adobe Photoshop, where the command is Layers>Flatten Image. Other software programs may use different terms. Look for a command to merge or stitch.)

❾ Use the crop tool to crop away any white space around your final image.

❿ Save your image and select the final image size (500 pixels x 500 pixels at 72 dpi is a good size for submitting pages to *Creating Keepsakes* or sending pages through e-mail). *Tip:* After stitching your image, it may not be exactly square. Fill in the height attribute and let the software program resize the width proportionately.

You're finished!

Troubleshooting Your Stitched Images

Still have problems with your stitched images? Here's a handy troubleshooting guide to help you resolve your stitching problems.

Problem: I have a hard time working with such large file sizes.
Solution: After you make your initial scans, reduce the file sizes by 50 percent so you can see the entire files on your computer screen. To reduce the file size in Photoshop, for example, I choose Image>Image Size. I then reduce the width and height of my image by 50 percent. For example, if my original image is 1600 x 1200 pixels, I change the dimensions to 800 x 600 pixels.

Problem: My scanner is too small, and it cuts off parts of my 12" x 12" pages.
Solution: Letter-sized scanners are only 11" long, and many legal-sized scanners will only scan 11.7", so a portion of your layout will be cut off unless you scan in four sections.

Scrapbooker Karen Burniston's solution? "I rarely go to the trouble of piecing four scans together, but I do pay careful attention to which edge gets cut off. I look for an

'unimportant edge' that won't affect the overall appearance of my layout," says Karen.

Problem: My final image looks blurry.
Solution: You've probably overlapped your images too much. The more one photo overlaps another, the harder your stitching software will have to work to match the images. A tip? When you save your final image, set compression and

Now that you know how to scan and stitch your layouts, you can share them electronically with *Creating Keepsakes*! You'll find current calls for pages at *www.creating-keepsakes.com/magazine/your_work*.

smoothing to zero to retain as much detail as possible (this may not be possible in all programs).

Problem: I have a hard time matching up my two images.
Solution: Set the zoom feature on your screen to 200%. You'll be able to find the merge point of your images more easily this way. *Tip:* Look at your lettering (both titles and journaling) for places where you can match up your images. Photo mats are another key place to match images.

Problem: I can see a clear line between my two images.
Solution: You may need to adjust the brightness between the two original images. One side of your layout may have scanned lighter or

darker than the other side. You can also use your eraser tool to remove or hide the line between both halves of your layout.

Problem: The colors on the two halves of my layout look different.
Solution: If it's an option, turn off "automatic color balancing." If you leave it on, this feature may adjust the color balance differently for each half of your layout (especially if you have a color on one side of your layout that doesn't appear on the other side).

Problem: I scanned my "lumpy" layout and I can see shadows on my final scan.
Solution: The shadows are caused by light "sneaking in" under the cover of

your scanner. Try scanning in a dark room to eliminate shadows.

Problem: When I scanned the two halves of my layout, one was bigger than the other. Now they don't match up when I try to overlap them.
Solution: After scanning both sides of your layout, click on each side and check the image size. Resize both images so they're the same height.

Scanning and stitching layouts is a skill that may require some patience and practice. Once you get the hang of it, you'll be scanning, stitching and sharing your pages electronically in no time at all! ♥

3 Hot Scanner Picks—Under $200

Interested in high resolution and advanced performance at an affordable price? These Canon, Epson and Hewlett-Packard models offer 48-bit color, easy operation, fast scans, quick previews and exceptional value.

CanoScan 5000F USB Flatbed Scanner
Up to 2400 dpi resolution
Built-in 35mm film adapter for slides and negatives. Exclusive dust/scratch removal technology.
www.canon.com

Epson Perfection 1660 PHOTO Flatbed Scanner
Up to 1600 dpi resolution
Built-in filmstrip adapter, easy connectivity, ColorTrue technology and automated 4-button scanning.
www.epson.com

HP ScanJet 4570C Flatbed Scanner
Up to 2400 dpi resolution
Professional-quality scanning, with lighted adapter for archiving, enlarging and reprinting negatives and slides. No warmup time!
www.hewlettpackard.com

Computer Corner

1 Art Inspiration

The other day, I thought of the famous Marilyn Monroe painting by Andy Warhol and decided to pattern a layout after it. I found a web site with prints of Warhol's work, then found a piece, "Che Guevera," that I liked even better. Using the colors in the original piece, I re-created a larger version of the painting that uses my photo as the subject.

Here's how I used Warhol's art to create the layout in Figure 1:

❶ I found a picture of me that had nice contrast in the face and hair. Next, I used the selection tool in Paint Shop Pro to highlight a certain section of my face. I copied and pasted this image into a new box and lowered the color depth to two colors: black and white. I then increased the color depth back to 16 million colors.

❷ Next, I used the color selection tool to identify the colors in the original face, hair and background section. I used the paint bucket to fill in the face, hair and background with these colors, then saved the photo and repeated this process for all nine pictures.

❸ After opening up a new, larger box, I pasted each photo in order into the new box, taking care to line up each photo perfectly. I printed the resulting image on high-quality, glossy photo paper, then trimmed it before adding it to my layout. I love how this technique lets you re-create the look of an art-museum poster.

—Lana Rickabaugh, Maryville, MO

2 Preservation Artist

With my computer and a blank address label, I can create a "signature" for my pages. To accomplish this, I insert a down-loaded, scrapbook-related graphic and type in *Scrapbooked by Tammy Herzog.* After I complete a page, I add the date to my label, pull it off the backing, and affix it to the back of my page. This way, future generations will know who the "preservation artist" was.

—Tammy Herzog
Fairmont, MN

custom photo looks

Create them in minutes on your computer

Let's face it. As scrapbookers, sometimes we struggle with photos that didn't turn out as planned. Other times we have a hard time customizing our photos without overdoing them. Here are three fun ways to alter your photos digitally.

Getting Started

Before we begin, you'll need photo-editing software. (See "Where to Find Photo-Editing Software" for programs you can buy for under $50.) Once you get the software, be sure to use your program's Help menu to find locations and instructions for certain buttons, toolbars and techniques.

When working with digital prints, remember: the higher the resolution, the better the print. Scan items at 600 dots per inch (dpi) or higher for the best quality. Select a higher dpi during scanning if you plan to enlarge the photo.

Figure 1. Use a pre-made border from photo-editing software to stylize your photos in seconds. *Photos by Anita Matejka and Amy Flakus.*

Border It

1 For a quick, easy, yet snazzy technique, use the pre-made borders or edges that come with your photo-editing program. For example, I like to apply different colors, textures and gradients to the pre-made borders in PhotoImpact by Ulead Systems. All I do is select and apply the look I want. For the photos in Figure 1, note how I used the same border but customized the colors.

BY ANITA MATEJKA

Figure 2. Remove an unwanted item in the background (such as the tree at right) by using a cloning tool. *Photos by Anita Matejka.*

Cloning

No, we're not talking about sheep cloning or anything of the sort. But, have you ever discovered that the photo you thought was perfectly composed has a distracting item in the background? (Maybe there's a clashing red ball, or a tree branch that looks as if it's growing out of your daughter's head.)

Photo-editing software has a feature called "cloning" that can help. With cloning, you can copy one part of an image to another area of your photo. You can use different clone tools to "paint" the copied image with any of several different styles and sizes of brushes. The cloning tool is also a great solution for cleaning up tears, scratches and other damaged portions of heritage photos.

To use cloning:

❶ Find the cloning tool on your toolbar (or in your Tools menu).

❷ Select the area you'll be cloning or copying from. For the example in Figure 2, I selected a spot in the clear sky. This was an easy photo to clone because the sky was all the same color.

As you experiment with cloning, start with simpler choices, then move on to more difficult, detailed photos as you gain experience. *Tip:* When working with skin tones, stay close to the area you're cloning over to keep the same tones.

❸ Select the size and shape of your cloning "brush." For areas with fine detail (such as those around the toes in Figure 2), select a smaller number or a finer brush point. For large, open areas, make the process faster by selecting a larger brush size. *Note:* When working with finely detailed areas, zoom in 200–400% to get a closer view of the area you're working on.

❹ Click and drag the mouse where you want to clone the image. Depending on the cloning tool you've selected, an image will gradually appear. You can set the size and transparency of the brush to modify this effect.

❺ To create a nicely blended look, clone from several different areas of your photo.

If you'd like to take your pictures to the next level, try the techniques above. You'll love the creative possibilities! ♥

Where to Find Photo-Editing Software

Want a good photo-editing program for under $50? Consider the following:

◆ **Ulead PhotoImpact** (*www.ulead.com/pi/runme.htm*). The 7.0 version works well, or you may want to spend a little more to get the latest version.

◆ **Adobe PhotoDeluxe** (*www.adobe.com*)

◆ **CorelDraw** (*www.corel.com*)

◆ **ArcSoft Photo Studio** (*www.arcsoft.com*)

Prefer to try before you buy? Visit these sites for trial programs:

◆ *www.hotfiles.com*

◆ *www.cnet.com*

◆ *www.tucows.com*

your problem solved!

Computer tips for working with text and photos

Figure 1. Create a watermark effect by printing your text on both your background paper and your photograph. *Page by Lana Rickabaugh.* **Supplies** *Patterned paper:* Karen Foster Design; *Vellum:* Hot Off The Press; *Embossing powder:* Stamp Affair; *Computer font:* Aquiline, downloaded from the Internet.

Text on Photos

For the page in Figure 1, I wanted the text to overlap the photograph and continue back onto the paper so it would look like a watermark. To create this look, I scanned in my photo and inserted a text box in my photo-editing program. I typed in my text and sized and arranged the text box so it overlapped the photo.

I then changed the text overlapping the image to a dark gray and printed it out on photo paper. I went back into my software program, removed the photograph, changed all the text back to black, and printed it out again on vellum. I then trimmed the photo to the edge and laid the photo over the vellum, being careful to line up the text.

—*Lana Rickabaugh, Maryville, MO*

BY LORI FAIRBANKS

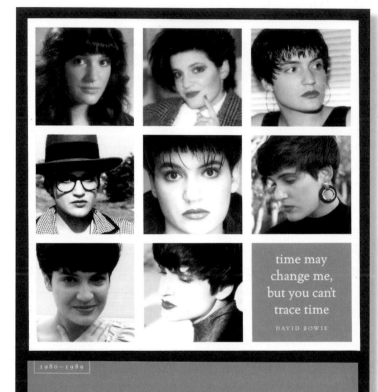

time may change me, but you can't trace time

DAVID BOWIE

1980—1989

a decade of evolution
and hair

How do you characterize a decade that began with Journey and hot-rolled hair styles and ended with R.E.M. and a lot less hair? When I think of the '80s, I think of one word: evolution. I went from 15 to 25 during the "me" decade, and certainly made myself the focus of those 10 years.

From an insecure girl who just wanted to be liked by everyone, to a woman who truly felt like she "became," the '80s was a one-way ride to self-awareness land. I was able to figure out a) who I was, and b) who I was not. And I'm not certain, but I think hair had a lot to do with it.

When the '80s began, I was a freshman in high school. Naive and insecure, perhaps, but I did have the requisite gear to fit in at the time: a fake lambswool coat; perfectly curled hair, courtesy of my Clairol hot roller set; purple eyeliner and a host of luscious lip glosses; and an appropriate music collection—Journey, Foreigner, and a little AC/DC thrown in to show I could rock.

Molly was my best friend and we moved freely from clique to clique, or at least I did. I was friends with everyone. From the preps to the rockers, Cathy was a girl who could blend.

All was sailing along smoothly in a sea of suburban conformity until the summer before my junior year when Molly had to go and start listening to new wave music. Strangely enough, I never knew that listening to songs like "Oh Mickey" by Toni Basil and "That's What I Like About You," by the Romantics would change the course of my life, literally.

It was the beginning of the end of normalcy when I chopped off the perfectly curled hair and began my love affair with short hair. Everything then was so tied into the music. Next came Duran Duran and Billy Idol. Then into the darker shades of new wave with Bauhaus and goth rock. Then into the cooler side of classic alternative music like David Bowie. I was hip and cool, or so I thought, and I got to make myself look any way that I wanted to. It was the epitome of liberation.

After then going on to college and living in Seattle a few years, I tired of the constant hip and cool of the Seattle scene, and packed up my bags for Texas. Time to regroup, focus on my education and move on with my life. My years in Texas were the missing piece of my life's puzzle. Time to really sort out all of the confusion and contradiction of being a 20-something.

By the decade's end, I was still me, only a better version, I think. One with more confidence. One with more calm. Molly was still my best friend, although the miles had long since separated us physically. In 1989, I met Dan, and we all know how that turned out. We often joke that if we'd met at any other time during the '80s, it just wouldn't have worked out for either of us.

So, here's to evolution, baby. I wouldn't trade a minute of the '80s. (Well, maybe about 8 months of it, but that's another story.) I still listen to Journey and feel like I'm 17, driving with Molly on a chilly spring day, windows rolled down in my Datsun B210, the heat cranked up, singing our hearts out to "Stone in Love," youthfully oblivious to the fact that we will one day grow up and out of a decade.

Converting Photos 2

Do you have a lot of photos you'd like to use on a layout that incorporate different colors, backgrounds, quality and periods of time? This is what I faced when trying to find images to use on a 1980s retrospective layout I wanted to create (Figure 2). My solution? Scan all of the photos into Adobe Photoshop, convert them to black-and-white images, and tweak the curves and contrast/brightness levels until all the photos have a similar visual quality. Taking a group of dissimilar photos and converting them to black and white is a great way to create visual unity on a layout.

Once I scanned all the images and saved them, I opened a new document with ½" page margins on all sides. I created three columns, with roughly ¼" gutter widths. I then made one picture box in an exact square (it spanned the width of one column) and duplicated it twice across the page. I then duplicated the row of three boxes two more times vertically down the page. This gave me nine photo boxes to drop in my various photos.

I used the ninth box to highlight a quote from a favorite song, changed the box fill to a green I had created, then highlighted the text and set the font color to white. I used this technique again to create the title block at the bottom of the page. I printed this sheet out on heavy weight photo paper and trimmed it to fit on a piece of black cardstock.

For the journaling block inside my layout, I took one image, enlarged it in Photoshop, and dropped it into a large picture box. I set the image color to green, then changed the color percentage from 100% to 30% to create a "ghosted" background image. This image adds a little texture to the journaling block, while still allowing the text to be easily read. I then added my journaling over the top of the image. Again, I printed this out on archival-quality matte paper, trimmed it and adhered it to the page.

—*Cathryn Zielske, St. Paul, MN*

Figure 2. Unify a variety of unrelated photos by changing them to black and white and sizing them. *Page by Cathryn Zielske.* **Supplies** *Photo paper:* Heavyweight Archival Matte Paper, Epson; *Computer font:* Celestia Antiqua, Adobe.

Figure 3. Rather than cut out intricate fonts, use your photo-editing software to create a custom title block. *Sample by Allison Strine.* **Supplies** *Patterned paper:* Hot Off The Press; *Punches:* EK Success; *Heart stamp:* Stampcraft; *Embossing powder:* Ultra Thick Embossing Enamel, Suze Weinberg; *Computer font:* Rough Brush, downloaded from the Internet.

3 Intricate Font Help

Sometimes I want to use a certain font on a layout, but it's so intricate that the font just can't be cut with a craft knife (even if I did feel like spending all day on the title—which I don't!). I've discovered a simple way to incorporate these fonts into my layout with my photo-editing software.

To make the title block integrate well with the rest of the layout, I first scan a piece of the patterned paper that I'm using elsewhere in the layout. Next I use the color picker to choose a dark shade of the patterned paper. I type in the title using this color.

I position this layer on the background to create the drop shadow. I then change the font color to white and type in the title again. I position it over the drop shadow and I'm done! I print out the title block, then embellish it to suit the page. The process is easy, and I get great results!

—*Allison Strine, Atlanta, GA*

4 Printing on Circle Tags

I wanted to print on metal-rimmed circle tags without having to cut or punch another piece of paper and adhere it to the tag. To do this, I printed my text on a sheet of plain white paper, held it to the light, and adhered my tag over the print with a Hermafix tab. I then sent it through my top-loading Lexmark Z22 printer. Believe it or not, the tag went through just fine! I've found that if I want to print more than one tag at a time, all I have to do is place the second tag about 3" down the page.

—*Donna Downey, Huntersville, NC*

5 Printing on Fabric

I just discovered a new technique: I run a sheet of cardstock through my Xyron machine, then adhere fabric to the cardstock. I can print words or pictures on the fabric by selecting "fabric sheet" from the Properties menu for my printer. I can now print on ribbon, then embroider the words and use them as embellishments on a layout. I plan to scan my baby's picture, then print it in black and white on a piece of fabric (cut from one of his outfits) to make my scrapbook cover.

—*Lisa Mabry, Chester, VA*

6 Letter Sticker in a Pinch

I like to use letter stickers on my layouts. It makes me crazy, though, when I still have a whole page of stickers but not enough of one letter to complete a project. I've found a great solution to use in a pinch.

Before I use the last of one specific letter, I scan it into my computer. I can then adjust it to match the actual size of the sticker letter and cut it out. It doesn't always exactly match the actual letter, but it usually works well enough to get me through the project. This tip sure helps when it's late at night and I need just one more letter to complete that page I've been working on!

Rest easy, sticker manufacturers—this doesn't prevent me from buying more stickers. For me, the whole point of stickers is to avoid needing to do the cutting and gluing myself.

—*Sue Thornton, Lynnwood, WA*

Discover a neat, new way to use your computer for scrapbooking? Tell us about it! Send your computer tip (and an electronic example if applicable) to *computertip@creatingkeepsakes.com.*

COMPUTER TIPS

Page by Beth Beyrer.
Supplies *Patterned papers:* 7 Gypsies, KI Memories and Making Memories; *Metal frame and metal-rimmed tags:* Making Memories; *Computer font:* 2Peas Tiny Tadpole, downloaded from *two-peasinabucket.com*; *Nails:* Chatterbox; *Other:* Small jewelry tag, glass pebble and ribbon. *Idea to note:* Beth edited the picture in Adobe Photoshop.

Selective Coloring

Looking for a fun way to add color to a specific portion of your photograph? Here's how I used Adobe Photoshop to bring out the yellow and blue reflections on my layout:

❶ I scanned a color picture into my computer, then changed the picture to black and white.

❷ I selected the eraser tool, then ran it over the boys' reflections. This brought the color back to the picture.

❸ When I was satisfied with my modifications, I printed the photo on a color printer.

—*Beth Beyrer, Rockville Centre, NY*

Paper Saver

I used to hate printing my journaling on a full piece of 8½" x 11" paper—it seems like such a waste to use an entire sheet of paper to print a small section of journaling. My solution? My new HP PhotoSmart printer has a section for 4" x 6" photo paper.

I discovered that I can also cut cardstock, vellum and textured paper, then feed it through the photo paper slot. I love being able to print on small sheets of paper. I can even use my paper scraps for my journaling!

—*Samantha Stevens, Columbus, OH*

ARTICLE BY RACHEL THOMAE

photo masking, fast formats and more

Figure 1. Use photo-editing software to create beautiful photo effects. *Page by Cheryl Barber.* **Supplies** *Patterned paper:* Hot Off The Press; *Vellum:* Paper Adventures; *Embossing powder:* PSX Design; *Computer fonts:* Scrap Mommy, "Lettering Delights" Vol. 1 CD, Inspire Graphics; Staccato 222BT, downloaded from the Internet. *Idea to note:* After printing on vellum, heat-emboss the words with clear embossing powder.

Photo Masking

I love using my computer to create titles and journaling and to manipulate photos. Figure 1 contains a photo made from a color Polaroid I took of my son Ryan four years ago. After scanning the picture, I manipulated it in Corel PhotoPaint, which let me use "masks" to blur the background. (I wanted to make Ryan and the butterfly the focus of the photo.) The masking feature also let me leave the butterfly in color while converting the rest of the photo to black and white.

—*Cheryl Barber, Malone, NY*

Computer Corner

2 Easy Font Access

If you have lots of computer fonts, you probably have to scroll through them to find the one you want. (And that's if you can remember its name!) I've discovered an easy way to access my scrapbooking fonts in Microsoft Word through the Style feature. Just follow these steps:

❶ Click on the "Format" button in the toolbar and choose "Style." When the Style window pops up, click on "New."

❷ Name the style, click on the "Format" box at the bottom of the window, and choose "Font." I create style names such as "Title CK Italic" or "Journal Cursive" to identify the font name and how I might use that style on my pages.

❸ Select the font and size you want defined for that style. Click on "OK" to close the Font window and "OK" again to close the New Style window.

❹ Click on "Organizer." Highlight the style you just created and click on "Copy" to copy it to Normal.dot. Click on "Close." *Note:* Be sure to copy every style you create to Normal.dot so the style will be saved for future use.

Now, whenever you open a file or create a new document, just click on "Format" and "Style." All the styles you've created will appear before you. If you want to see only those styles you've created, select "User-Defined Styles" in the List box. Click on "Apply" and you're ready to type in your text. I've found this system much easier to use than scrolling through hundreds of fonts.

—*Janet Taddeo, Menlo Park, CA*

3 Mini-Calendars for Layouts

At the beginning of each month, I make a calendar on my computer. I put in special events like holidays, birthdays and vacations. I save a copy, then print it out and hang the calendar on our schoolwork/art wall in the kitchen. Every day, I record something we've done (such as putting up the tree or making cookies for Christmas).

At the end of each month, I access the calendar on my computer and type in the events I've written in by hand. I print the calendar out and decorate it with stickers. Next, I scan the calendar and shrink it to approximately 4" x 5" so I can print four calendars on one sheet of paper.

I use the mini-calendars to remind our family what we did each month. I also put a copy in each son's scrapbook. I usually group the mini-calendars by season: winter (January, February and March); spring (April, May and June); summer (July and August); and fall (September, October and November). December gets its own layout as the introductory page for Christmas.

—*Virginia Lincoln, Glen Rock, NJ*

4 Patterned Paper in a Pinch

When it's late and I don't have the paper color or pattern I need, I use my computer to print out a swatch on light-colored cardstock or vellum.

I can print out textured looks as well. Recently, I printed a small section of woodgrain paper to create a "fence" look for paper piecing. After chalking it to add "dimension," the fence looked quite realistic.

—*Nannette Coffey*
Aurora, CO

5 Intact Edges

When scanning a small item, instead of placing it at the edge of the scanner, use a clear ruler or a small, clear triangle ruler to align it. This will move your item toward the center of the scanner, keeping the shape and size perfectly intact.

—*Rebecca Odom*
Ft. Walton Beach, FL

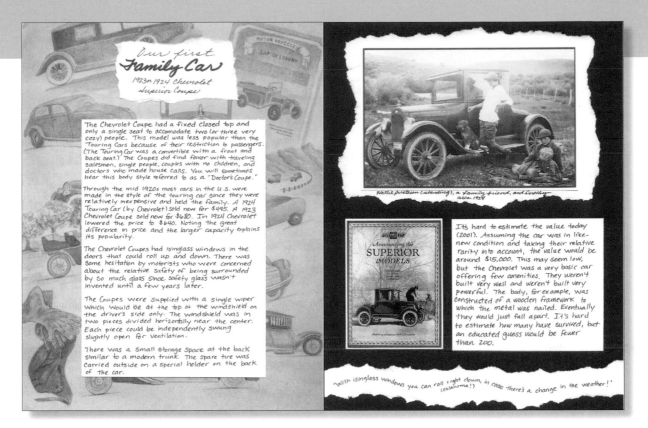

Figure 2. Find information about items in old photos by conversing with enthusiasts who frequent special-interest message boards. *Pages by Dayna Gilbert.* **Supplies** *Patterned paper:* NRN Designs; *Chevy ad:* Downloaded from the Internet; *Pen:* Zig Writer, EK Success.

6 Special-Interest Groups

Are there elements in your family photos that you'd like to know more about? Ever wondered when a photo was taken? Search the Internet for special-interest groups!

As I've worked on my heritage album, I've tried to learn more about the cars and motorcycles shown in my early family photographs. I've searched online for message boards about classic Chevrolets, international trucks and vintage motorcycles.

Whenever I've found an active message board (with questions and answers added in the past 24 hours), I've posted my questions, along with a link to my photo. I've also left my e-mail address. Because some people post replies directly to the message board, I've been diligent about keeping track of when and where I've left messages.

I've learned more than I ever expected. My best find has been information about my family's first car (Figure 2). I came across a man online who is restoring a similar model. He told me all about the make, model name and year, original cost, how the car operated and more. He was thrilled to share his information with me. It's amazing what can be learned from photos!

—*Dayna Gilbert, McMinnville, OR*

7 Fast Formats for Layouts

I look through magazines and find layouts that really appeal to me. Next, I duplicate the formats in my AppleWorks drawing program. I just drag boxes of different sizes and shapes and place them where I want them.

When my format is complete, I print it or save it to my computer's hard drive. When I print the format, I place my photos over the boxes and add my own embellishments. I can get any layout to work for any occasion, and I don't have to spend time thinking up new formats for layouts.

—*Sherry Bluemel, Lyman, WY*

Computer Corner

8 Printing on Scraps

I do all of my journaling and most of my titles on my computer. Even though I always print out a test page to check for dimensions and spelling, once I output my text on cardstock, it seems I always find a typo or change my mind about wording.

I've found that I can use removable double-sided tape to temporarily attach appropriate-sized scraps of cardstock to my test page and resend it through the printer. When I reprint the corrections, I can use up my scraps, avoid generating new "scraps," and even print on several different colors with just one additional pass through the printer. Removable double-sided tape is a great time and paper saver!

—Vicki Reisenfeld, El Dorado Hills, CA

9 Backup CDs

I scan all my layouts into my computer and electronically "burn" them onto CDs. I include as many layouts as I can on each CD, saving them in chronological order and labeling them. I then make an additional copy of each CD.

One copy stays in our fire-resistant safe at home, while the other is at my husband's office. This way, should our home ever be ruined by fire, flood or another disaster, the memories I've worked so hard to preserve in albums will be saved. With the new printers that can output 12" x 12" pages, I'll simply reprint the pages I've spent so much time creating.

—Bridget Grieme, Delta Junction, AK

10 Printing Clip Art

Even with all the great clip-art CDs and free downloads online, I was disappointed with how the images looked when I printed them. I get higher color quality now by using photo paper with a matte finish instead of using regular white paper or cardstock.

—Robin Poupard, Highland, CA

11 Saving Mom's Handwriting

While creating a scrapbook of my childhood, I came across many special photos of me as a young child. My mother had done a terrific job documenting the details of each photo—unfortunately, they appeared on the backs of the photos.

I wanted to preserve these details in my mother's handwriting, so I scanned her notes and printed them on archivally safe paper. I then placed her notes next to the photos in my scrapbook.

—Robyn McKay, Olathe, KS

confessions of a fontaholic

Learn how to download and manage fonts

The right font, whether downloaded or from a software package, can lend artistic effect and help reflect a layout's theme. *Pages by Karen Burniston.* **Supplies** *Patterned paper:* Mary Engelbreit, Creative Imaginations; *Fibers:* Rubba Dub Dub, Art Sanctum; *Vellum:* Paper Adventures; *Punches:* Marvy Uchida; *Eyelets:* Rubber Baby Buggy Bumpers; *Circle cutter:* Creative Memories; *Computer fonts:* Smash (title) and 1942 Report (journaling), both downloaded from *www.free-typewriter-fonts.com. Idea to note:* Karen applied a shadow effect to the word "Flicker" before outputting it.

You know how some people like to collect things? I have an aunt who's been collecting rusty old spoons for 40 years. I used to look at her and feel relieved that I didn't clutter up *my* life by acquiring lots of unnecessary stuff.

Wait a minute. I guess that's not entirely true. I do collect something—fonts! In fact, my computer is overflowing with hundreds of luscious, original and funky fonts. I'm a fontaholic, and I don't want to be cured. Are you a fontaholic, too? Take the fun quiz on page 274 to find out.

→

BY ALLISON STRINE

Computer Corner

Fontaholic Quiz

Want to pin down whether you're a fontaholic or not? Simply ask yourself if you've ever:

◆ spent hours searching the Internet for the "perfect" handwriting font when you've already got 17 of them installed?

◆ tried to impress a date by telling him the restaurant menu was written in Minya Nouvelle?

◆ seen the font in an ad at a theater and been shushed for crying out, "Hey, that's Fabulous '50s Normal!"

◆ recognized the font they use on "Jeopardy"?

◆ used the phrase "Girls Are Weird" and had it not refer to your teenage daughter?

If you answered yes to any of the above, you too are a fontaholic. If you're not a fontaholic, fear not. There's hope for you yet!

Common Font Questions

Part of becoming a fontaholic is knowing where to find fonts and how to use them. To help initiate those of you who are not fontaholics yet, I've provided answers to the following common font questions:

Q Where in the world can I find computer fonts?

A Where in the world *can't* you find them? Fonts come in all shapes and sizes, and you can find them in software packages and online at all kinds of web sites. While some web sites offer fonts for free, others make them available for purchase (or they provide a mix of both).

You can find plenty of sites that spe-cialize in fonts. Just type the word "font" or "free font" in your search engine, and you'll be inundated with enough choices to keep you happy for a long time! Prices range from "free to a good home" to upwards of $20 per font. Some of the best web sites even divide their fonts into groups like "Famous Fonts" (fonts from movies or TV) and "Typewriter Fonts" (see Karen Burniston's layout on page 273).

Tip: Know the name of a certain font but not sure where to find it? Go to *www.fontseek.com*, type in the font name, and you can often discover where the font is located online or in a software package.

Q Okay, I found a really cool font. How do I download it?

A You need to do three things. First, make a new folder to put your downloaded fonts in (you only have to do this once). Second, download the font. Third, unzip and install it. Sound scary? Don't worry—I'll hold your hand! Just fol-low these steps:

❶ Make a new folder by clicking on "My Computer" on your computer desktop. Double-click on the C: drive. From the "File" menu, select "New" and choose "Folder." Give your folder a distinctive name so you can find it later.

❷ Go to the web site that contains the font you want to install. Click on the font icon to select it. A window will appear, prompting you to choose "Open" or "Save to Disk." Choose "Save to Disk" and hit "OK." Follow the prompts to save the

5 Quick Tips on Font Design

When including fonts on scrapbook pages, keep the following in mind:

❶ It's best to stick with two or three fonts at most on a layout.

❷ Repeat a font elsewhere in the layout for visual interest.

❸ Choose a legible font for journaling. Save the wild ones for large titles.

❹ Mix things up a little by using one font for the title and a different one for the subtitle.

❺ Basic black is nice, but don't forget that you can print your fonts in a variety of colors.

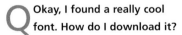

4 STEPS TO DOWNLOADING A FONT
(see detailed instructions above)

❶ Make a folder to store your font in.

❷ Download the font.

❸ Unzip it.

❹ Move the font to the Fonts Folder in "My Computer" on your desktop.

Free Font Finds

Today's font packages offer great choices, yet sometimes you want something a little different. Free downloadable fonts could be just what you're looking for!

Following are six fresh fonts that can be downloaded by visiting *www.dafont.com/en.* Simply note the easy download-ing instructions on-screen, then enter the desired font name in the Search box and conduct your search. When the font appears, download a Windows version, Macintosh version, or e-mail the font to a friend.

file to your font folder. Now you have the font on your computer, all "zipped" up in a tidy but unusable file.

❸ Unzip your file. Huh? Most fonts are squished into tiny files to conserve space and make transferring simpler. To use the fonts, you have to uncompress or "unzip" them. To do this, you need a program called WinZip (or ZipIt for the Macintosh). WinZip can be downloaded at *www.winzip.com.*

Double-click on the little zip icon in your fonts folder. Follow the prompts to unzip the file, which will appear in its own window.

❹ Click on "My Computer," then "Settings," then "Control Panel." Open the Fonts Folder in the Control Panel, and drag the font icon to the Fonts folder. Sometimes you need to reboot your com-puter before it knows that the new font is there. This process may seem time-consuming at first, but believe me—soon you'll practically be able to do it in your sleep!

The right font, whether downloaded or from a software package, can lend artistic effect and help reflect a layout's theme.

Computer Corner

Q My computer is running too slowly. Could the 400 fonts I've got loaded in my system be a factor?

A Yes! Having more than 250 fonts loaded at any one time can affect your computer's happiness. You don't have to permanently delete the extras, though. You just need a font management program to help you uninstall fonts.

Q Help! I have hundreds of fonts, all of them wonderful, but I can never find the one I want. I feel overwhelmed and out of control. How do I get organized?

A My dear, you are in dire need of font management software. As the name implies, these programs let you organize and categorize your fonts. One popular program, The Font Thing, is available at *http://members.ozemail.com.au/~scef/tft.*

html. The Font Thing is nice because it's free, but it isn't the most user-friendly program around. It may or may not be the best option for people.

My personal favorite is the CK Font Organizer that's built into the new "Fresh Fonts" CD by *Creating Keepsakes.* With the Font Organizer, you can install and uninstall fonts without deleting them from your computer. You can have fun sorting your fonts into categories like "Kid Fonts" and "Script Fonts." You can print font samples and view sample text in your choice of colors. Another big plus? A "help wizard" walks you through the whole daunting process of getting started.

Q Are there some fonts that I shouldn't delete?

A Yup. Don't delete the fonts that Windows needs to run. Any font that has an MS or a red "A" at the beginning of its icon is a must-have. Don't delete the Arials, Couriers, Symbols or Times New Romans, either. If you're ever not sure whether it's "safe" to remove a font or not, check the following web site: *http://pagemakersupport.adobe.com/ adobeknowbase/root/public/pm1010.htm.*

Q Should I back up my fonts in case my computer crashes?

A It depends. Don't bother if you enjoy spending countless hours reloading software. If not, you'll definitely want to make a copy of the font folder and save it somewhere else, such as a writeable CD or another storage medium (such as a ZIP drive or FLASH card).

Q I want to share a font with my online friend. How can I do this?

A First, be aware that it's illegal to download or distribute by e-mail a font that is not freeware. To e-mail a font, simply attach it (from the fonts folder) to the e-mail. The recipient will be able to save and install the font as explained above.

Q I am a diehard Mac user. Can I play with fonts too?

A Of course. You can even find a program at *http://www.dafont.com/en* to convert PC fonts to Mac fonts. Have fun!

Share your favorite computer tips!

Discover a neat, new way to use your computer for scrapbooking? Tell us about it! Create a great layout using your tip? We want to see it! Simply attach your scan as a .JPG file (under 500K, please) and send your computer tip to us at *computertip@creatingkeepsakes.com.*

I f you've read this far, you might as well face it—you're addicted to fonts. Now I want to see you download 30 new fonts this week! But first, repeat after me:

I am a fontaholic

I am a fontaholic

I AM A FONTAHOLIC

I AM A FONTAHOLIC!

No fonts were harmed in the making of this article. ♥

3 favorite font effects

Flip, go gray and mix with flair

Figure 1. Achieve a distinctive, dry-embossed look in three steps, shown on page 278. *Samples by Merrilynne Harrington.* **Supplies** *Patterned paper:* Making Memories and Paper Adventures; *Vellum:* Paper Adventures; *Eyelets:* Making Memories; *Computer fonts:* CK Elegant, CK Hustle, CK Lumpy (mirrored for word "wonderful") and CK Stenography, "Fresh Fonts" CD, *Creating Keepsakes;* *Adhesives:* 3L Corp. and Tombow.

Isn't the holiday season great? From Thanksgiving to New Year's, I get together with family and friends for fun festivities and fabulous food. I savor the tried-and-true dishes that are family favorites, plus I sample new recipes my mom's discovered in *Martha Stewart Living* magazine or on a cooking channel. (If all goes well with a "trial" recipe, as evidenced by an empty serving dish at the end of the meal, Mom may add the recipe to her repertoire for our next holiday get-together.)

When following a recipe, it's good to use the "tried and true" and experiment for a little variety. The same holds true for computer fonts. Enjoy the existing options, such as color and style, but don't stop there. With a little effort and know-how, you can create a feast of cool font effects. Here's how to create three of today's favorite looks.

Flipping or "Mirroring" a Font

It's common nowadays to use computer fonts for titles, journaling or accents. As I've taught classes at Creating Keepsakes University and scrapbook conventions, students have inevitably asked a familiar question: "How do I flip fonts?" They want to be able to print words in reverse on the back of cardstock or patterned paper. This allows them to cut a word out quickly and not worry about the letter outlines showing on the front.

To flip or "mirror" a font:

❶ Select a word processing program, such as Microsoft Word. (If you don't have Word, access your program's help file under the Help menu and search for the keywords "mirroring" or "flip image.")

❷ Load the cardstock or patterned paper upside-down in your printer, so your lettering will print on the reverse side of the sheet.

❸ Locate the toolbar in Microsoft Word. Select Insert, Picture, then WordArt.

❹ Choose a WordArt style (outline, no fill).

BY MERRILYNNE HARRINGTON

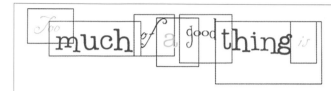

Step 1: Use text boxes in Microsoft Word (see page 280 for instructions) to create a cool, multi-colored title. Output it on vellum.

Step 2: Create the word "wonderful" in WordArt and select blue as the outline color. Fill the letters electronically with the desired shade of blue. Output the word on cardstock and cut out the individual letters.

Step 3: Create a second copy of the word "wonderful" in WordArt. Remove the fill color and change the outline color to black. Flip the word, keeping a horizontal orientation. Output the word, then use the image as a pattern to emboss the word on vellum.

---

❺ Select a TrueType font style and size. Type some text, then click OK.
❻ Select Draw from the Picture Toolbar, then Rotate or Flip, then Flip Horizontal.

Shortcut: If the font to be flipped is from one of the "Best of Creative Lettering" CDs by *Creating Keepsakes*, you can bypass the steps above. The software's popular Fliplettes feature handles the procedure in a single step.

Try this:

Once you've mastered the basics of flipping a font, experiment with the following:

◆ Print your flipped letters on the back of cardstock or patterned paper. (You can also print on a copy of a photograph.) Cut each letter out to create a custom die-cut letter. Layer it with a variety of papers. Add emphasis by matting the letter with paper in a coordinating paper.

◆ Create a dry-embossed pattern by printing the flipped letters on the back of regular copy paper. For the title in Figure 1, I used the printed font as a guide and embossed onto vellum with a stylus. (I had previously used the text box technique shared later to print part of my title in color on the same sheet of vellum.) I then discarded the

pattern and flipped the vellum over. I accented the word "wonderful" by placing colored letters in the same font behind the embossing.

◆ Print on the back of cardstock and use the flipped font as a sewing guide. Hand-stitch the outline of the font, then flip your paper over. Fill in the center of each letter with chalk, rub-ons or colored pencils. You can also fill your font in with a coordinating color of cardstock, vellum or patterned paper.

◆ Extend the techniques above to clip art as well as fonts. You'll love the clever coordinating accents you can create for your scrapbook pages!

Gray-t Expectations

Not only is gray type easy on the eye, it's indispensable when you need a subtle guide for custom lettering looks and accents. To create it:

❶ Select a word processing program, such as Microsoft Word. (If you don't have Word, access your program's help file under the Help menu and search for the keywords "font color," "font format" or "format text.")

❷ Type your text, then select the portion you want to change by highlighting it.

❸ To select the color gray, click the arrow next to the Font Color button, then select the desired shade. To apply the color used most recently, click Font Color on the Formatting toolbar.

Try this:

Once you've colored your text gray:

◆ Trace over it with a pen, colored pencil or paint. I love to use watercolor pencils and a blender pen.

◆ Position craft wire over it, using the gray letters as a guide. Once you've recreated each letter with wire, stitch the letter onto your page with clear thread.

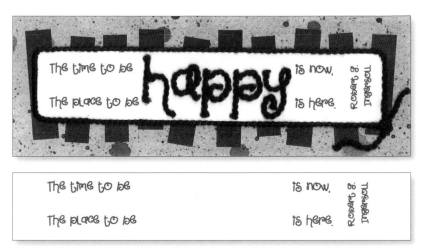

Figure 2. Output a word in gray, then adorn the letters with fiber, beads and other accents. *Samples by Jennifer Ditz.* **Supplies** *Patterned paper:* Doodlebug Design; *Computer font:* 2Peas Girly, downloaded from *www.twopeasinabucket.com*; *Other:* Fiber.

◆ Use it as a sewing guide. (You don't need to flip your font first.) If you'll be using a backstitch technique (so all your stitches run together without any space showing between), you can print the font on the front of your paper. Just be sure to print in the lightest possible shade of gray.

Stitch over the gray portion of letters with embroidery floss, thin-gauge wire, metallic thread or even ribbon. Dress up your stitches by stringing on beads, sequins or charms. When sewing on paper, it's usually a good idea to create

a sewing guide by piercing your paper with a needle. This little trick guarantees perfect stitches most of the time!

◆ Print out your letter or word. Apply an adhesive (such as Zig Two-Way Glue by EK Success or Wonder Tape by Suze Weinberg) within the outline.

Note how in Figure 2 scrapbooker Jennifer Ditz printed the word "happy" in gray, then covered it with fibers to create a simple yet elegant look. You can extend this idea by adding other mediums such as glitter, rhinestones, sequins or beads.

A Faster Way to Fabulous

You may be the adventurous sort who loves to manipulate fonts—or you may prefer a program that does it for you. Be aware that some software packages offer cool effects you can achieve with the click of a button or two. For example, the following looks are available in Photo Express – My Scrapbook Edition by Ulead Systems (*www.ulead.com*):

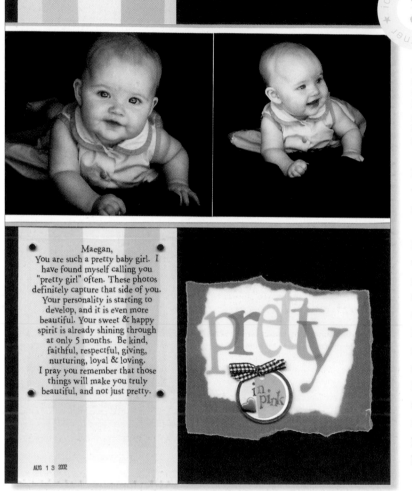

Figure 3. Use the WordArt feature to create title letters that look like they're made of vellum. *Page by Amy Grendell.* **Supplies** *Patterned paper:* Colorbök; *Vellum:* Keeping Memories Alive; *Rubber stamps:* PSX Design ("in pink") and Staples (date); *Computer font:* Garamouche ("pretty" and journaling), Impress Rubber Stamps; *Ink pad:* Clearsnap; *Eyelets:* American Tag Co. (silver) and Making Memories (heart); *Ribbon:* Impress Rubber Stamps.

Maegan,
You are such a pretty baby girl. I have found myself calling you "pretty girl" often. These photos definitely capture that side of you. Your personality is starting to develop, and it is even more beautiful. Your sweet & happy spirit is already shining through at only 5 months. Be kind, faithful, respectful, giving, nurturing, loyal & loving. I pray you remember that those things will make you truly beautiful, and not just pretty.

AUG 1 3 2002

Mixing Font Spacing, Styles and Sizes

How can today's scrapbooker use a multitude of text styles and sizes? Text boxes! With them, you can group letters, words or lines of text into "containers" that can be moved and sized on your page.

You can also use clip art, graphics and AutoShapes to achieve fun font looks. If you're someone who avoids fonts because they look too formal and "computerized," think again. It's easy to change a font look by altering the placement of a character, a word or an entire phrase.

To mix your font spacing, styles and sizes, follow these steps:

❶ Select a word processing program, such as Microsoft Word. (If you don't have Word, access your program's help file under the Help menu and search for the keywords "text box," "drawing object," "graphics" or "AutoShape.")

❷ Add a text box to your document by double-clicking on the text box icon on the drawing toolbar. Or, select Insert from the menu bar and choose the Text Box option. Click the document to insert the text box.

To resize the text box, drag its sizing handles until the box is the size you want. Position the text box by dragging it to the desired location.

❸ Type your text within the text box. Change the font style and size by highlighting the text and selecting a new style and size from the drop-down menus on the formatting toolbar. To open the font dialog box, select Format from the menu bar. (Depending on the font style and size you choose, you may have to resize your text box accordingly.)

Tip: To display a word vertically, size the text box so it's only wide enough for one letter. This will force the other letters to wrap and stack vertically on top of each other.

❹ Continue to add a text box for each word in your title. Size each box accordingly and click and drag it to the desired position on your page.

A few notes about text boxes: They're best explained by comparing them to small squares of cardstock. Like cardstock, text boxes will overlap when they're layered on top of each other (or too closely together). This will cause some of your text to disappear from sight.

To change the order of your text boxes and make the text visible, click on the text box that's overlapping another element. Right-click on the text box and select Order, then select Send Behind Text. This should send the text behind the other box so all of the words are visible.

5 By default, each text box has an outline. Don't worry—the outline is easy to remove! Simply right-click on the text box and select Format Text Box. Select the Colors and Lines tab, then click on the drop-down menu under "Line" and select No Line.

Try this:

Once you're comfortable with text boxes, customize them as follows:

◆ Alter the look of just one word by changing your character spacing in the Font Format menu.

◆ Use text boxes to create pop-out journaling. Insert a text box with a new font style or color in your journaling text.

◆ Layer your letters or make some semi-transparent. In Figure 1, I used text boxes to create part of my title. In Figure 3, Amy Grendell used WordArt to layer each of the letters in the word "pretty." (Each letter is a separate image created in WordArt.) To imitate the look of vellum, Amy changed the density of some letters to semi-transparent.

◆ Add a graphic or a piece of clip art to your text. If your title includes the letter "o" (such as "Snow" or "Love"), replace it with a snowflake or heart image. Work with the graphic just as you would a text box, changing the order to make sure all the letters and graphics are visible.

Figure 4. Tap your imagination and create cool tag effects with AutoShapes, WordArt and innovative products. *Page by Karen Burniston.* **Supplies** *Patterned papers:* Carolee's Creations; *Computer fonts:* Carpenter ICG (background of tags) and Bobtag ("Emma"), downloaded from the Internet; *Mesh:* Magic Mesh, Avant Card; *Photo corner rubber stamp:* Moe Wubba; *Ink pad:* Clearsnap; *Embossing powder:* Stampendous!; *Dotlets:* Doodlebug Design; *Other:* Fibers.

◆ Ready to try something a little more advanced? Take a closer look at Figure 4, where Karen Burniston used WordArt and AutoShapes in Microsoft Word to create the appearance of layered tags. First, Karen chose a "scribbled words" type font (Carpenter ICG) that had a big height difference between caps and lower case. She typed random words in it, alternating upper and lower case. Next, Karen clicked on the editing tool in WordArt that makes all letters the same height. This resulted in illegible words that could be rotated and used to create interesting text backgrounds.

To create her tags, Karen used AutoShapes to layer a trapezoid on top of a rectangle. Next, she overlaid a circle with white fill and made it 25 percent transparent to mock vellum. To mimic a metal edge, Karen used a doughnut AutoShape, colored gray. A no-fill, no-line text box was used for each black letter.

Karen printed her tags on glossy white cardstock. She then printed a second set, changing the background color to black, and layered it behind the brown tags.

Whether you have a basic word processing program or high-end software, the custom looks above are within your reach. Flip, go gray and mix letters with flair. You'll be a font guru before you know it! ❤

Mix and

Even small letters can be sensational

Figure 1. Stack your word strips down the side of your layout. *Page by Becky Higgins.* **Supplies** *Patterned paper:* Scrip Scraps; *Reindeer accent:* Li'l Davis Designs; *Letter stickers:* Pioneer Photo Albums; *Letter stamps:* Hero Arts; *Computer font:* Courier, Microsoft Word; *Pens:* Pigma Micron, Sakura; *Chalk:* Stampin' Up!; *Square grommet:* Westrim Crafts; *Metallic thread:* Kreinik; *Pop dots:* All Night Media; *Eyelets:* Doodlebug Design.

BY BECKY HIGGINS

Ever feel like the titles on your layout overwhelm your pictures? Ever feel like

they take up too much precious space? You're not alone! While the obvious

"fix" is to create smaller titles, these tend to be "lightweight" visually. They

may fit the available space, but they don't pack much visual punch.

I've got a fun twist that can help! By "mixing and matching" elements of your title, you can provide the visual variety your title needs. Another bonus? Mix-and-match titles work well with virtually any set of pictures, regardless of theme or the subjects' age or gender. I'll walk you through the process.

STACKING AND COMBINING

Even though the party layout in Figure 1 has a lengthy title, note how confined it is on the left side. By mixing and matching my letter styles and word strips, I was able to stack them on top of each other. I combined computer fonts, stickers, stamps and even my own handwriting. I added journaling below the strips.

You can mix and match titles and journaling in several ways. (I've provided a variety of examples in Figure 2.) Simply try your hand with alphabet stamps, computer fonts and letter stickers (I especially love the tiny ones). Mix and match letter styles, including print and cursive versions of your handwriting.

PRESENTING

Now comes the fun part! In Figure 3, I've shown how to create different looks with different methods. You're free to select whatever works best for you. When scrapbooking with vellum, use a glue stick or clear adhesive or try adding eyelets, brads, or grommets instead. At times, I roll a strip of cardstock to add dimension to my pages.

To add definition to my titles, I

STAMPS

Computer Fonts

stickers

Mix and match letter styles

handwriting

cursive

Figure 2. Try some of these approaches in your mix-and-match titles.

Figure 3. The custom looks above will keep you inspired for many pages to come!

add a torn block of paper and daub a little chalk around the edges. When I crumple a strip of paper, I like to adhere it to my page with brads or eyelets that can handle the extra texture.

I like to use plain blocks or strips of cardstock as well. One variation is to take a strip and wrap craft or kitchen foil around it. In Figure 3, I elevated the foil strip with pop dots. I created word strips with paper yarn and raffia. I cut cardstock crookedly for special effect.

KEEPING IT SIMPLE

You can be colorful—or not—with your mix-and-match title. For example, Figure 4 shows a simple color scheme of black, white and foil (very "boy," don't

you think?). Note how I simplified the look by using my hand-writing only. I also avoided including stickers, stamps or computer fonts.

Unlike the layouts shown previously, Figure 5 presents a different display of word strips. Instead of incorporating stacked, aligned letters, the newborn baby's name and birth information are almost "scattered" along the top of the layout. I mixed and matched the use of pens, stickers and stamps for greater effect.

Next time a small title needs "pow," put the mix-and-match technique to work. It's a fast, simple way to add sophistication and style to your scrapbook pages! ♥

Figure 4. Simplify your look by using only one or two colors in your title. *Photos by Tina Allgaier, journaling by Tyler Allgaier, page by Becky Higgins.* **Supplies** *Brads:* American Pin & Fastener; *Foil:* Reynolds; *Pens:* Zig Millennium, EK Success.

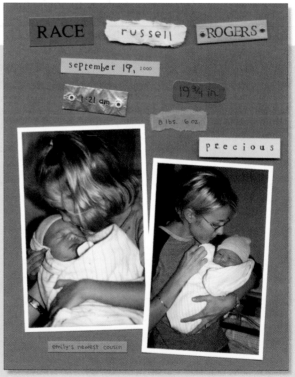

Figure 5. Use lots of color and a "scattered" look when presenting bits of information about a birth, person, place or event. *Photos by Nanci Jarman, page by Becky Higgins.* **Supplies** *Letter stickers:* Pioneer Photo Albums; *Letter stamps:* Hero Arts (lowercase), PSX Design (uppercase); *Pen to write on foil:* American Crafts; *Other pens:* Micron Pigma, Sakura; *Pop dots:* All Night Media; *Eyelets:* Magic Scraps; *Brads:* American Pin & Fastener.

the main event

No pictures? No problem!

Figure 1. It's OK to devote an entire album to one event. You don't even need pictures. *Album cover by Rebecca Sower.* **Supplies** *Album:* Paper Chase; *Fibers:* Adornaments, EK Success; *Rubber stamps:* River City Rubber Works (electric fan), Limited Edition (postcard) and unknown (alphabet); *Embossing enamel:* Suze Weinberg; *Metal-rimmed tag:* Making Memories; *Pen:* Zig Writer, EK Success; *Other:* Ceramic tiles.

Creating a layout for an event can be so much more than a play-by-play of the occasion. Put your heart into it.

"IT'S MY PARTY, AND I'LL CRY IF I WANT TO!" Actually, it was my daughter's party, but I was the one crying when the photographs didn't turn out. I accept full blame. I was determined to try my father-in-law's fully manual SLR camera, and I didn't think I needed to read the manual. Ha! When my photo developer handed me 36 sheets of 4" x 6" glossy black paper, I thought my life was ruined.

As is often the case in these less-than-perfect moments, I learned a lesson and discovered something else. Suppose those failed photographs had turned out beautifully. Would I have created a layout that simply included photographs, a little summary journaling, and the who, what, when stuff? Probably. But, *because* the photos were a disaster, I went into more detail and included more background about the celebration.

For the birthday event, I created a miniature scrapbook (see page 287). It dawned on me that I could really soup up my other event lay-

ARTICLE BY REBECCA SOWER

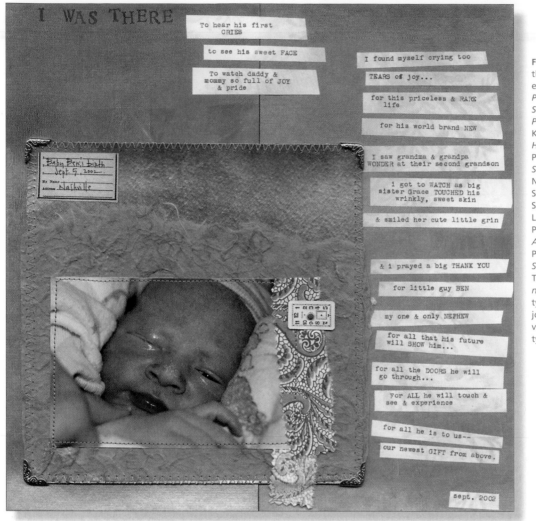

I WAS THERE

To hear his first CRIES

to see his sweet FACE

To watch daddy & mommy so full of JOY & pride

Baby Ben's Birth
Sept. 5, 2002
My Name
Address Nashville

I found myself crying too

TEARS of joy...

for this priceless & RARE life

for his world brand NEW

I saw grandma & grandpa WONDER at their second grandson

i got to WATCH as big sister Grace TOUCHED his wrinkly, sweet skin

& smiled her cute little grin

& i prayed a big THANK YOU

for little guy BEN

my one & only NEPHEW

for all that his future will SHOW him...

for all the DOORS he will go through...

For ALL he will touch & see & experience

for all he is to us— our newest GIFT from above.

sept. 2002

Figure 2. Put a little heart into your event journaling. *Page by Rebecca Sower.* **Supplies** *Patterned paper:* K & Company; *Handmade paper:* Provo Craft; *Sticker:* Nostalgiques, Sticko by EK Success; *Paints:* Lumiere, Jacquard Products; *Alphabet stamps:* PSX Design; *Stamping ink:* Tsukineko. *Idea to note:* Rebecca typed her journaling on a vintage Corona typewriter.

outs (you know, the ones *with* photos) by applying this failed-photo strategy.

After you have revisited and retold an event without any photographs to support it, the events you scrapbook will take an amazing leap forward. Here are a few tips to add vitality to your event journaling.

Life after Pictures

I was so excited to be present at my precious nephew's birth several months ago. If I had taken the typical journaling approach, I would likely have told about all the activity—how long I waited at the hospital, the family's excitement, and how cute my nephew looked in his little stocking cap.

Instead, I chose to document the event by writing down some of my private musings from that day (Figure 2). This is my way of giving my nephew a little piece of my heart. I'm conveying on a layout what I felt about that very special occasion (and it's *obvious* he's adorable in his stocking cap!).

Put Your Heart into It

I know I suggest this exercise often, but look through your completed layouts. Focus on the event-based ones this time. Read the journaling. Does it have heart? Or does it simply give a play-by-play of the activities? It takes minimal effort to turn event journaling from blasé to meaningful. It just takes a little heart.

Does your journaling have heart? Or does it simply give a play-by-play of the activities?

Figure 3a. An event with no photos or disappointing photos still deserves attention. *Mini album by Rebecca Sower.* **Supplies** *Patterned paper:* EK Success (edges) and Karen Foster Design (watercolor); *Beads:* Blue Moon Beads; *Pen:* Zig Writer, EK Success; *Binding system:* Tozicle, CARL Mfg.; *Other:* Buttons, slide holder, paper clips, craft wire, lace, embroidery floss and ribbon.

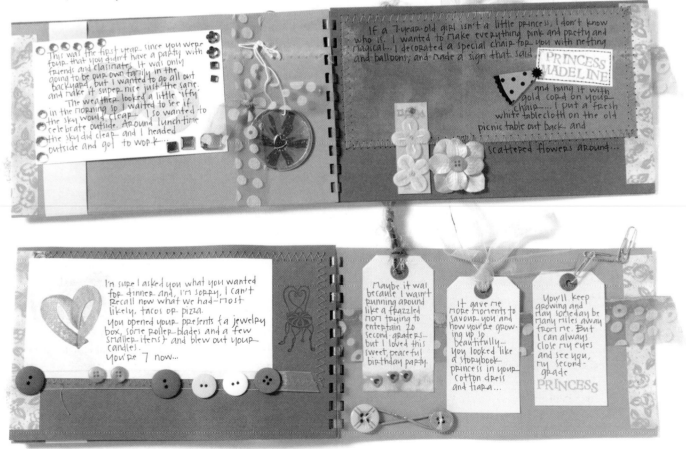

Figure 3b. Present your memories and thoughts of an occasion in a lovely, loving way. *Pages by Rebecca Sower.* **Supplies** *Patterned paper:* EK Success (edges) and Karen Foster Design (watercolor); *Rubber stamps for chair and alphabet:* PSX Design; *Eyelets:* Making Memories; *Pen:* Zig Writer, EK Success; *Watercolors:* Winsor & Newton; *Stamping ink:* Tsukineko; *3-D embellishments:* Jolee's by You, Sticko for EK Success; *Paints:* Lumiere, Jacquard Products; *Tags:* Impress Rubber Stamps; *Fibers:* Adornaments, EK Success; *Binding system:* Tozicle, CARL Mfg.; *Other:* Buttons, paper clips, rhinestones, artificial flowers, brad, embroidery floss and ribbon.

143

Figure 4. Don't just recap an event in play-by-play journaling. Let your subjects know how important they are to you. *Pages by Rebecca Sower.* **Supplies** *Pen:* Zig Writer, EK Success; *Sticker:* Nostalgiques, Sticko for EK Success; *Photo corners:* Canson; *Labels:* Avery; *Embroidery floss:* DMC; *Other:* Pencil, notebook paper, envelope flap, buttons, artificial flower, ribbon, paper clip, bookplate, brads, fabric, dictionary excerpts, staples and necklace.

For example, children have been heading off for their first day of school for many years. But as every mom can attest, the first day of school for *your* child is different. It's *your* child! Write the "first day of school" recaps and include what your heart is feeling. You're giving your child another nice reminder of just how special he or she is to you (see Figure 4).

This exercise works for just about any event. Include more emotions as you recount the occasion.

(Don't) Lean on Me

Don't use your photographs as a crutch! This is especially tempting when we're scrapbooking photos from years (or in my case, *months*) ago; you know, the ones where you would hardly remember being there if weren't for the photos.

Here's an example: You have a photo of your daughter grinning at you from atop a pony. It's easy to journal something like: "Emily had so much fun riding the ponies at the pony party." Or, easier yet, I could find a cute quote or saying that fits well with the photo and let that serve as my journaling (and you *know* how much I love quotes).

Still, if we use photographs (or even quotes) as crutches for our journaling, we're missing the point. Try this exercise. Look at a photo, then close your eyes. You probably won't believe the random thoughts that come to mind about the event.

Here's a more heartfelt journaling example for that pony party: "Fear or fun? I wasn't sure how Emily would react to her first pony ride. But when her turn came, you would've thought she'd been jumping on ponies all her life—all three years of it. Being scared would've been understandable. A lot of kids are. But Emily? Well, she just

approached the animal like she does most situations in life—with no apprehension at all. Watch out, world—here comes Emily!"

Think Big

Sometimes a bigger event, such as a family vacation or Christmas, warrants a separate album. Instead of trying to sort through, narrow down and accommodate a limited number of photos, why not create an album for that event? (See album on page 287.) If you're a die-hard chronological scrapbooker, you can still stay on course. Simply dedicate a page or two in your regular album to the event and include a small note about the special album.

Is it important to journal your events? Absolutely! When you include thoughts from your heart along with the event's recap, you're remembering the best of both worlds. ♥